First published in 2007 by Egmont UK Limited
239 Kensington High Street, London W8 6SA

™ & © Warner Bros. Entertainment Inc.
Harry Potter Publishing Rights © JKR. (s07)

ISBN 978 1 4052 3310 1
1 3 5 7 9 10 8 6 4 2
Printed in Italy

# Harry Potter

This book contains photos and posters of spectacular scenes from the first five Harry Potter films. Relive your favourite wizard's most magical adventures so far . . .

## Poster Annual 2008

# Beginnings

Albus Dumbledore, Hogwarts' Headmaster arrives
at Privet Drive, with his Put-Outer.

Albus Dumbledore and Minerva McGonagall deliver baby Harry Potter
to the Dursley house.

Dozens of mysterious letters fly down the chimney of number four,
Privet Drive.

Rubeus Hagrid delivers baby Harry to Dumbledore.

Harry must get through the barrier at platform nine and three-quarters, to board the Hogwarts Express.

Harry is happy to see Hagrid at Hogsmeade station.

A fleet of boats carries first-year students to Hogwarts castle.

# Hogwarts, Year One

Draco Malfoy is Sorted into Slytherin.

Harry, with his snowy owl, Hedwig - a birthday present from Hagrid.

Harry and Ron play a game of wizard chess.

The first flying lesson with Madam Hooch.

**GRYFFINDOR**

Hermione Granger is a talented and studious witch.

Seamus Finnegan doesn't have much luck in Charms class.

Harry listens as Oliver Wood explains Quidditch.

Harry with Gryffindor Quidditch captain, Oliver Wood, before the
first match of the year.

Hogwarts caretaker Argus Filch, with his cat, Mrs Norris.

Hagrid prepares to hatch a dragon egg.

Draco Malfoy   Harry Potter

Stuttering Professor Quirrell is the Defence Against the Dark Arts teacher in Harry's first year.

Hermione knows the right spell for every occasion.

**Gryffindor wins the House Cup!**

**The Great Hall erupts in celebration.**

# Hogwarts, Year Two

The new school term begins with a bump for Harry and Ron . . .

. . . as they crash Mr Weasley's flying car into the Whomping Willow!

Ron looks horrified when he receives a Howler!

The gushing Gilderoy Lockhart is the new Defence Against the Dark Arts teacher.

Draco Malfoy is the ruthless new Slytherin Seeker.

Dobby visits Harry
in the hospital wing.

Harry's classmates during their first Duelling Club meeting.

Hermione brews
Polyjuice Potion.

Ron and Harry drink the disgusting the Polyjuice Potion.

The chamber of Secrets has been opened. enemies of the heir ... beware

Filch accuses Harry of Petrifying his cat, Mrs Norris.

Harry 'enters' the past through Tom Riddle's diary.

Harry defeats the Basilisk using Godric Gryffindor's sword.

Dumbledore's phoenix, Fawkes, heals Harry with its tears.

Tom Riddle disappears when Harry uses the Basilisk fang to destroy the diary.

GRYFFINDOR™

Harry Potter

# Hogwarts, Year Three

Harry takes the Knight Bus to Diagon Alley.

The *Daily Prophet* reports that Sirius Black has escaped from Azkaban Prison.

Dementors attack the Hogwarts Express.

Professor Lupin is the new Defence Against the Dark Arts teacher in Harry's third year.

Neville's Boggart takes the form of Snape . . . in Neville's grandmother's clothes!

Harry meets Buckbeak the Hippogriff in Care of Magical Creatures class.

Harry learns that Peter Pettigrew is alive.

Harry tries to save his godfather, Sirius, from the Dementors.

Harry and Hermione use the Time-Turner to save Buckbeak and Sirius.

Snape protects Harry, Ron and Hermione from Lupin's werewolf form.

Sirius is an Animagus, who can transform into a black dog.

Peter Pettigrew transforms back into a rat and escapes.

Harry conjures a Patronus to save Sirius from the Dementors.

Sirius Black is imprisoned at Hogwarts.

THE INTERNATIONAL ASSOCIATION OF QUIDDITCH™

PRESENTS

THE 422ND QUIDDITCH WORLD CUP

The GRAND FINAL

QUIDDITCH™ WORLD CUP STADIUM

DATE MOON IN PIS

THE GREATEST EVENT of the YEAR

# Hogwarts, Year Four

Venus in Leo · Ed. 240274

## SEEKER WEEKLY

INTERNATIONAL
Quidditch Magazine

### WORLD CUP

I.Q.A · 422nd WORLD CUP · INTERNATIONAL
ASSOCIATION OF QUIDDITCH

ENGLAND
LUXEMBOURG
USA
BULGARIA
INDIA
PORTUGAL
UGANDA
JAPAN

BRAZIL
SCOTLAND
IRELAND
SPAIN
FRANCE
ARGENTINA
PERU
AUSTRALIA

### GREAT FINAL

### BULGARIA vs. IRELAND
SPECIAL EDITION · ALL YOU NEED TO KNOW

Before term begins, the 422nd Quidditch World Cup takes place.

Death Eaters wreak havoc on the World Cup campsite.

The Goblet of Fire rejects the Weasley Twins' attempt to enter the Tournament.

Dumbledore announces the selection of the Triwizard champions.

Fleur Delacourt is the Triwizard champion for Beauxbatons.

Viktor Krum is the Durmstrang Triwizard champion.

Cedric Diggory places his name into the Goblet of Fire.

Harry awaits the first task of the Triwizard Tournament.

Professors attend the Yule Ball.

Hermione and Viktor dance at the Yule Ball.

Cho Chang attends the Yule Ball with Cedric Diggory.

Ron and Harry do not appear to be enjoying themselves at the Yule Ball.

The Hungarian Horntail dragon.

Harry and Hermione celebrate Harry's completion of the second task of the
Triwizard Tournament.

Harry in the
enchanted maze during
the third task.

The Triwizard Cup ends up
being a Portkey.

Harry is trapped by a statue
in the graveyard.

Harry returns from the graveyard with Cedric's body.

Harry is devastated by Cedric's death.

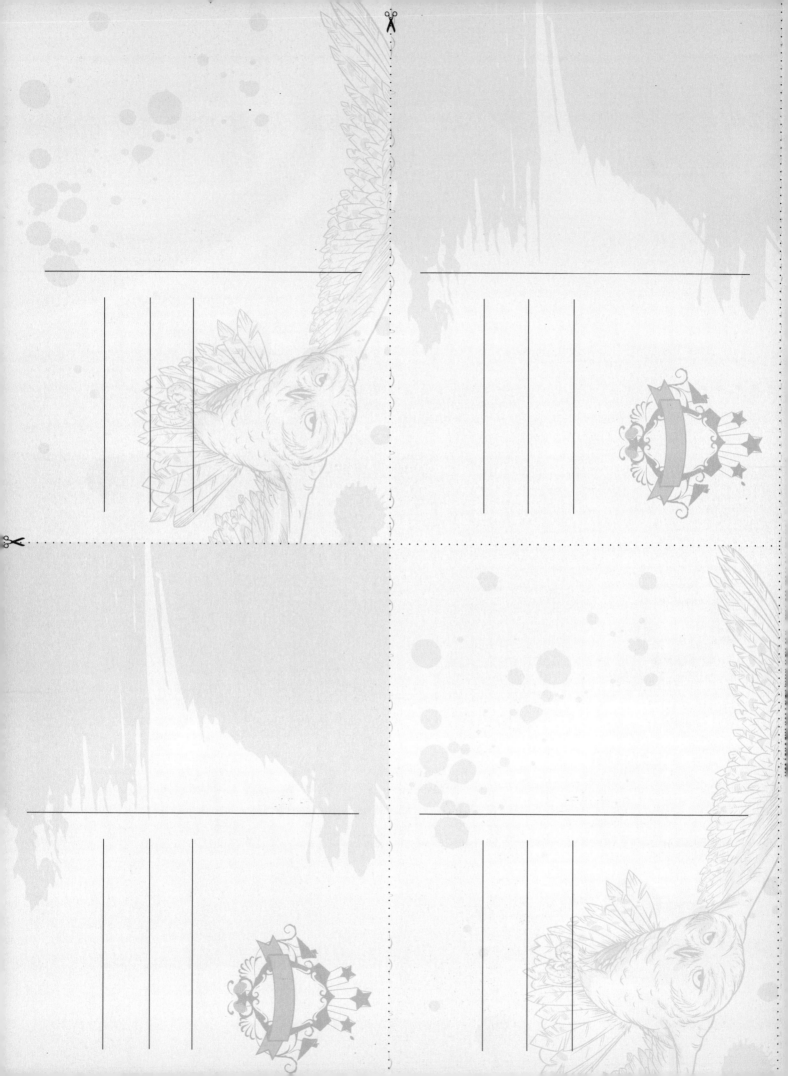

POTTER

Viktor Krum

Fleur Delacour

# Hogwarts, Year Five

Harry defends himself and Dudley against the Dementors.

Harry spots his cousin Dudley and his pals coming towards him.

Dudley Dursley becomes quite ill after an encounter with the Dementors.

Harry is comforted by his godfather, Sirius.

Sirius tells Harry that he is a good person to whom bad things have happened.

Harry attends his hearing at the Ministry of Magic.

Harry, Ron and Hermione listen to Hagrid discuss his visit with the giants.

Professor McGonagall reads the *Daily Prophet*.

Harry waits by the Gryffindor fireplace, hoping to hear from Sirius.

Professor Umbridge, the new Ministry-appointed Defence Against the Dark Arts teacher.

Umbridge makes Harry do lines with her special quill.

Dumbledore insists that Harry study Occlumency with Snape.

Members of the D.A. practise their defensive spells.

Dumbledore's Army.

Harry helps Cho with her defensive spells.

Harry's first Occlumency lesson with Professor Snape.

Harry awakes from a vivid nightmare.

Hermione insists that Harry tell Dumbledore about Umbridge's detention.

Harry and Cho share their first kiss.

The Gryffindors are not happy when Umbridge becomes Hogwart's new Headmistress.

Umbridge oversees the O.W.L.s – 'Ordinary Wizarding Levels'.

Luna Lovegood's father is the editor of the *Quibbler*.

PROCLAMATION.

EDUCATIONAL DECREE
№ 98

THOSE WISHING TO JOIN THE
INQUISITORIAL SQUAD
for EXTRA CREDIT
May sign up in the
High Inquisitor's
OFFICE

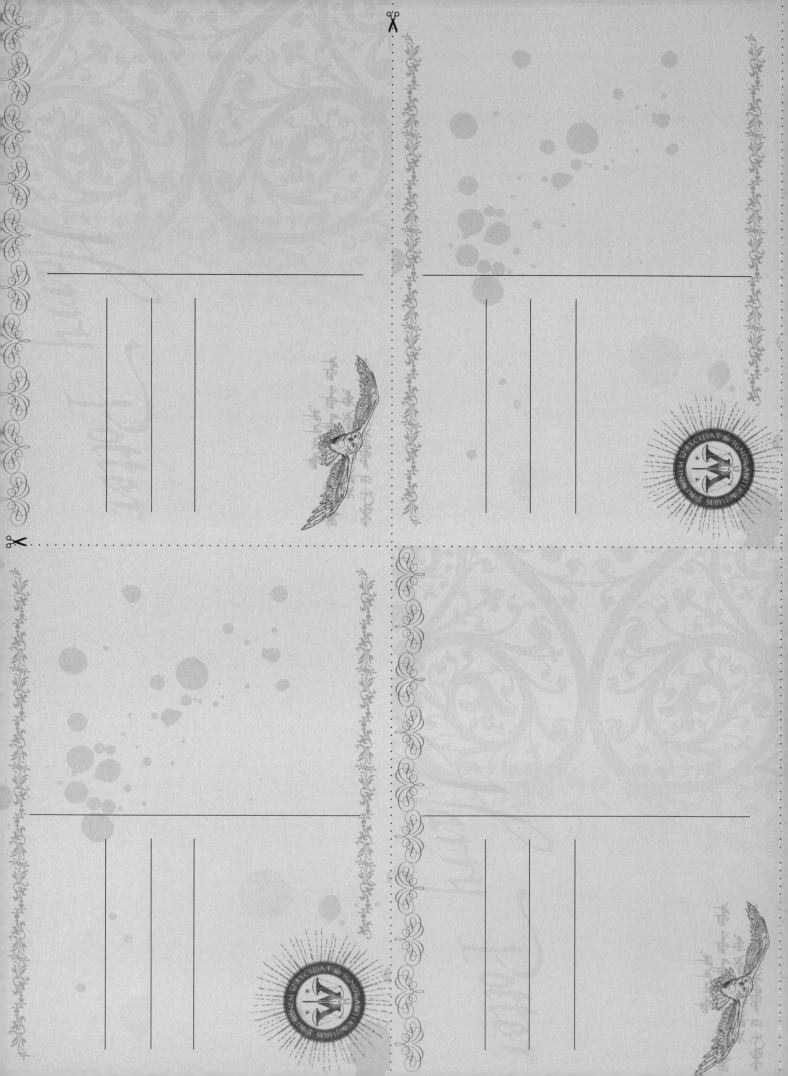

Grawp

Hermione is worried about Harry.

Harry refuses to give up the prophecy.

Sirius battles Death Eaters in the Department of Mysteries.

Dumbledore apologises to Harry for keeping him in the dark for so long about Voldemort.

*Harry Potter and the*
# THESTRALS

# THE FORBIDDEN FOREST